what's eating you?

a workbook for teens with **anorexia, bulimia** & other **eating disorders**

TAMMY NELSON, MS

Instant Help Books
A Division of New Harbinger Publications, Inc.

Publisher's Note

This publication is designed to provide accurate and authoritative information in regard to the subject matter covered. It is sold with the understanding that the publisher is not engaged in rendering psychological, financial, legal, or other professional services. If expert assistance or counseling is needed, the services of a competent professional should be sought.

Distributed in Canada by Raincoast Books

Instant Help Books
A Division of New Harbinger Publications, Inc.
5674 Shattuck Avenue
Oakland, CA 94609
www.newharbinger.com

Cover design by Amy Shoup

Printed in the United States of America

ISBN-13: 978-1-57224-666-9

The Library of Congress has cataloged the trade edition as:

Nelson, Tammy.
What's eating you : a workbook for teens with anorexia, bulimia, and other eating disorders / Tammy Nelson.
p. cm.
Includes bibliographical references and index.
ISBN-13: 978-1-57224-607-2 (pbk. : alk. paper)
ISBN-10: 1-57224-607-3 (pbk. : alk. paper) 1. Eating disorders in adolescence--Popular works. I. Title.
RJ506.E18N45 2008
618.92'8526--dc22

2008003617

12 11 10

10 9 8 7 6 5 4 3 2 1

First printing

table of contents

introduction

This book is about the prevention and treatment of eating disorders in teenagers. Every year, thousands of young girls develop eating disorders and eating disorder behaviors. Why? Because our culture holds standards of perfection that most of us will never achieve. We live in a very competitive society. We all want to be perfect. Some of us work harder at it than others, and some of us kill ourselves trying to get there.

Our media portrays a visual ideal of women that has nothing to do with what the average woman looks like. Yet girls as young as ten are trying to look like supermodels, actresses, and pop stars. No matter what the ideal in our culture is, girls will try to meet it, and the ways they choose—dieting, overexercising, purging, and other behaviors—are often self-destructive. Girls who are still growing have nutritional needs that dieting deprives them of. They need food, and lots of it, to be healthy and emotionally happy. When they deny themselves adequate amounts of food, their minds and their muscles starve, sometimes with devastating results.

Overeating, or compulsive eating and obesity, is another problem in our culture today. Eating too much food when you are not hungry is an emotional issue, not a hunger issue. People may eat simply because it tastes good, and in our society that's okay sometimes. Everyone uses food to celebrate holidays, birthdays, and other special occasions. But using food to take care of their need for love, attention, and affection puts people's physical and emotional health at risk; they need to find other ways to care for themselves.

Bingeing, or eating an extreme amount of food in a short period of time, is one type of overeating. People who binge may then purge, or try to get rid of the food they've eaten. There are different ways to purge; all are dangerous and unhealthy and can lead to self-destructive eating patterns.

Using this book, you will work on how to eat in healthy ways and how to stay in balance, physically and emotionally. You'll learn about eating behaviors that are dysfunctional, and you'll learn how to deal with stress and frustration that might otherwise lead to eating disorders. Feeling good about your body is also an important part of your health, and many of the worksheets deal with improving your body image.

Each worksheet includes these sections:

Focus

This section lets you know the issues the worksheet will address.

Exercise

Each exercise is organized in easy-to-follow steps. You can complete many of them right in this book, or you may want to copy them so that you can do them more than once. You'll also find a list of special materials, such as drawing paper or glue sticks, needed for the exercise.

Follow-Up

After each exercise, there are questions or points to help you think about what you've just learned. If you need additional space, you can use the pages provided for notes at the end of this book, or you may want to write your answers in a separate journal.

More to Think About

Here you'll find additional exercises to do after you finish a worksheet, or further ideas to think about. There may also be additional questions you can answer in a journal.

Many of these exercises may bring up a mix of emotions. You might feel sad, mad, or scared. You may react physically, feeling nauseated, jumpy, nervous, or tense. One good thing to do is to write about these feelings, using your journal or the space provided for notes. Remember, also, to tell someone else how you feel. Talk to your therapist, your parents, or a trusted friend. Your school counselor, social worker, or principal may also be able to help. There are also many websites where you can get information about eating disorders, depression, and anxiety.

The goal of this book is to help you be balanced and happy, and ultimately, to love and accept yourself exactly as you are.

eating disorders and body image

Did you know that if the typical mannequins you see in store windows were real women, they would be too thin to menstruate, or that if Barbie dolls were real, they would have to walk on all fours because of their physical proportions? Are you aware that twenty years ago, models weighed 8 percent less than the average woman, while today they weigh 23 percent less?

According to a recent National Women's Health Report, seven million American women have eating disorders. The facts and figures below, published by the Council on Size & Weight Discrimination, illustrate how widespread eating disorder behaviors have become and how great a gap there is between reality and the body types idealized by the media:

- The average American woman is 5′4″, weighs 140 pounds, and wears a size 14 dress.
- The "ideal" woman—portrayed by models, Miss America, Barbie dolls, and screen actresses—is 5′7″, weighs 100 pounds, and wears a size 2.
- One-third of all American women wear a size 16 or larger.
- 75 percent of American women are dissatisfied with their appearance.
- 50 percent of American women are on a diet at any one time.
- Between 90 percent and 99 percent of reducing diets fail to produce permanent weight loss.
- Two-thirds of dieters regain the weight within one year. Virtually all regain it within five years.
- The diet industry (diet foods, diet programs, diet drugs, etc.) takes in over $40 billion each year and is still growing.
- Quick weight-loss schemes are among the most common consumer frauds, and diet programs have the highest consumer dissatisfaction of any service industry.
- Young girls are more afraid of becoming fat than they are of nuclear war, cancer, or losing their parents.

- 50 percent of 9-year-old girls and 80 percent of 10-year-old girls have dieted.
- 90 percent of high school junior and senior women diet regularly, even though only between 10 percent and 15 percent are over the weight recommended by the standard height-weight charts.
- Girls develop eating and self-image problems before drug or alcohol problems; there are drug and alcohol programs in almost every school, but no eating disorder programs.

a look at your eating behaviors 1

focus

This exercise will help you understand healthy eating and a healthy body image. You'll learn about behaviors that may lead to eating disorders, and you'll look at your own eating behavior.

Healthy eating is eating what you want when you are hungry and stopping when you are full. You recognize what you crave and let your body have what it needs, including a balance of fruits, vegetables, protein, dairy products, and carbohydrates. You allow yourself treats for special occasions or just because you feel like it sometimes. You don't deprive yourself of any food group or particular food because you think it is "bad." You look at food primarily as a pleasant way to fill your body with fuel so it can function at its highest capacity.

You have a healthy body image when you are comfortable with your size, shape, and body parts. You wear clothes that flatter your shape, and you are relaxed about how you move. You don't compete with other women or feel bad about yourself when you think you are less attractive than another woman or than the cultural stereotype. You have few, or no, negative thoughts about your body.

Some of the more common eating disorder behaviors are listed below. As you read the list, think about your own eating behavior. On a scale of 1 to 10 (1 = not at all, 5 = often, and 10 = always), circle the number that best describes you.

I have excessive control over the way I eat.

1 2 3 4 5 6 7 8 9 10

I ignore my body's signals of hunger or fullness.

1 2 3 4 5 6 7 8 9 10

I eat when I feel strong emotion instead of when I am hungry.

1 2 3 4 5 6 7 8 9 10

I focus totally on food and eating.

1 2 3 4 5 6 7 8 9 10

Food and eating take up all my time.

1 2 3 4 5 6 7 8 9 10

My daily living activities are affected by either eating or restricting food.

1 2 3 4 5 6 7 8 9 10

I allow my weight and body image to interfere with my relationships.

1 2 3 4 5 6 7 8 9 10

I allow thinking about eating or not eating to interfere with my relationships.

1 2 3 4 5 6 7 8 9 10

My weight and body image interfere with my taking part in normal activities.

1 2 3 4 5 6 7 8 9 10

I struggle constantly for perfection in dieting, body image, or weight.

1 2 3 4 5 6 7 8 9 10

I have lost or gained a large amount of weight in a short period of time.

1 2 3 4 5 6 7 8 9 10

I am overly concerned with weight loss.

1 2 3 4 5 6 7 8 9 10

I weigh myself on a scale more than once a week.

1 2 3 4 5 6 7 8 9 10

I have strict rules about how much food I eat.

1 2 3 4 5 6 7 8 9 10

I have food taboos, such as, "I shouldn't let foods from different food groups touch each other on my plate."

1 2 3 4 5 6 7 8 9 10

For a long time, I have been strict about what foods I eat.

1 2 3 4 5 6 7 8 9 10

I compensate for taking in too many calories by exercising.

1 2 3 4 5 6 7 8 9 10

I vomit or use laxatives to help me lose weight.
1 2 3 4 5 6 7 8 9 10

I eat large amounts of food in a short period of time without wanting to.
1 2 3 4 5 6 7 8 9 10

I do not realize when I have eaten too much.
1 2 3 4 5 6 7 8 9 10

When I binge, I lose track of how much I've eaten.
1 2 3 4 5 6 7 8 9 10

I forget to eat for days at a time.
1 2 3 4 5 6 7 8 9 10

I eat only diet foods and diet drinks for days at a time.
1 2 3 4 5 6 7 8 9 10

I am usually dissatisfied with my appearance.
1 2 3 4 5 6 7 8 9 10

I am always dieting.
1 2 3 4 5 6 7 8 9 10

I use diet drugs and herbal supplements to help me lose weight.
1 2 3 4 5 6 7 8 9 10

I think about having gastric bypass surgery or liposuction.
1 2 3 4 5 6 7 8 9 10

I lie about my weight to my friends and parents.
1 2 3 4 5 6 7 8 9 10

I have at least three different sizes of clothes in my wardrobe.
1 2 3 4 5 6 7 8 9 10

Even at my lowest weight, I am not satisfied with what I weigh.
1 2 3 4 5 6 7 8 9 10

follow-up

Look over your responses to this exercise and consider these suggestions:

- If you circled 5 or higher for more than two statements, you may be on your way to developing an eating disorder. You may need help and should learn more about eating disorders.
- If you circled 5 or higher for more than four statements, you are definitely at risk of developing an eating disorder. Talk to an adult—parent, teacher, counselor, or doctor—right away.
- If you circled 5 or higher for more than five statements, your health may be in danger. You should seek medical attention.

more to think about

- What eating disorder behavior on this list can you change?
- How will you change that behavior in a healthy way?
- Which behavior do you think you will have a difficult time changing? Why?

your past and future 2

focus

This exercise will make you aware of when your eating disorder behaviors began and help you plan for a healthier future.

At ten years of age or older, girls enter a stage called puberty and begin to develop into young women. Puberty brings a lot of emotional and physical changes that sometimes trigger eating disorder behaviors. Thinking back to your past, can you identify the first time you recognized some of the signs of an eating disorder?

When was the first time you were embarrassed about your body?

___

When did you first restrict the type of food you ate because you were aware of how it might affect your body?

___

When did you first weigh yourself without a parent or doctor present?

___

Do you remember the first time you controlled your portion size?

___

When was the first time you tried a diet food, including soda?

___

When was the first time you binged? What did you binge on?

___

When was the first time you purged after a binge? How did you do it?

___

Now that you are older, look at what you can change that may help you in your growth over the next ten years. Choose one or more of the commitments below and decide on a period of time for which you will keep that commitment, no matter what.

I will not weigh myself for ____.
Instead, I will judge the size of my body by how I feel in it.

I will not drink diet soda for ______________________________________.
Instead, I will drink water or other healthy beverages.

I will not eat diet foods or go on a diet for _____________________________.
Instead, I will listen to my body and eat in a way that is healthy for me.

I will not overexercise to get rid of calories for ___________________________.
Instead, I will exercise for health and relaxation.

I will not binge for ____.
Instead, I will talk about or write about my feelings first.

I will not purge for ____.
Instead, I will tell someone that I have overeaten and feel scared and anxious.

follow-up

Share your commitment with someone you know, making that person aware that you may want to talk about your feelings.

I will share this commitment with _____________________________________.

more to think about

- How do you think you have changed since your eating disorder behaviors began?
- How do you feel about keeping this commitment?

draw your feelings 3

focus

This exercise will help you deal with stress. It will help you be more creative about looking at your problems and more realistic about how you see yourself.

Most people don't think in words; they think in images. As a human being, your mind is a collection of pictures and memories, storing images like a camera. Those images are connected to the part of your brain that collects smells, tastes, and sounds. When you smell fresh bread, for example, you may see a picture of your grandmother baking. Emotions work the same way, attached to an image in your mind. For example, if you feel angry, what mental picture do you see?

Sometimes, expressing your feelings in images can be easier than describing them in words. In this exercise, you are going to draw how you feel. The exercise is not about creating beautiful art; it is about communicating how you feel.

what you'll need

Colored pencils or thin markers
Two large sheets of drawing paper

Think about your mood for a moment. Do you feel like drawing in dark, bold colors or soft, pastel colors? Choose colors that you are drawn to, and make lines and shapes that seem to match your feelings. Are you feeling open? Boxed in? Sharp and edgy? Soft and mushy?

1. Using only lines, shapes, and colors, draw how you are feeling. As you draw, don't think about what you are drawing—let your feelings take over.
2. Using a new sheet of paper, draw how you would like to feel, again using lines, shapes, and colors.

follow-up

Answer the following questions:

How are your drawings similar? ______

How are they different? ______

Do you notice anything about the drawings that surprises you? ______

What did you learn about your feelings in this exercise? ______

How did drawing these pictures make you feel? ______

more to think about

Every day this week, take a few moments to draw how you feel. Notice what your choice of colors, shapes, and lines says about the day-to-day similarities and differences in your feelings. Pay attention to your eating disorder behaviors too. As you become aware of your behavior, look at your drawing. Can you make a connection between your feelings and your eating disorder behaviors?

boundaries and barriers 4

focus

This exercise will help you understand the difference between boundaries and barriers, and how they affect your relationships with others.

Your personal boundary is an imaginary line you draw around yourself to protect you from something you feel threatened by. If the threat is real, that boundary is important for your self-protection. But what if the threat is imagined or left over from the past? Then your boundary becomes a barrier, and it is probably harmful, rather than helpful.

The emotional distance you keep between yourself and other people is an indication of how safe you feel with them. The people closest to you are the ones you feel least threatened by, and you can let them into your inner thoughts and feelings. With other people, you may need to set better boundaries. Do you ignore your own needs to help others? Are you constantly focused on helping other people with their problems instead of working on your own? Do people take advantage of you?

Can you identify your boundaries? Do you put actual space between yourself and others? Do you withdraw from your friends and family, keeping your opinions and thoughts to yourself? Do you barricade yourself in your room? Do you hide behind alcohol or drugs?

And what about food? Or extra weight? Extra weight can sometimes be a barrier that we think we need in order to protect ourselves against something we perceive as a threat. Without that weight, we might be afraid of being too vulnerable to the dangers we see around us.

As you do the following exercises, keep in mind the difference between a barrier and a boundary.

1. Around this outline, draw a line that indicates a boundary that is a comfortable personal space for you. Indicate the thickness of that boundary and its shape and texture. Next, around the line you have drawn, use a different color to draw a boundary that indicates where you want to keep your peers and others that you are not sure you trust. Finally, draw a boundary that shows where you want to keep people you don't trust. Make sure you indicate the thickness or texture of that line.

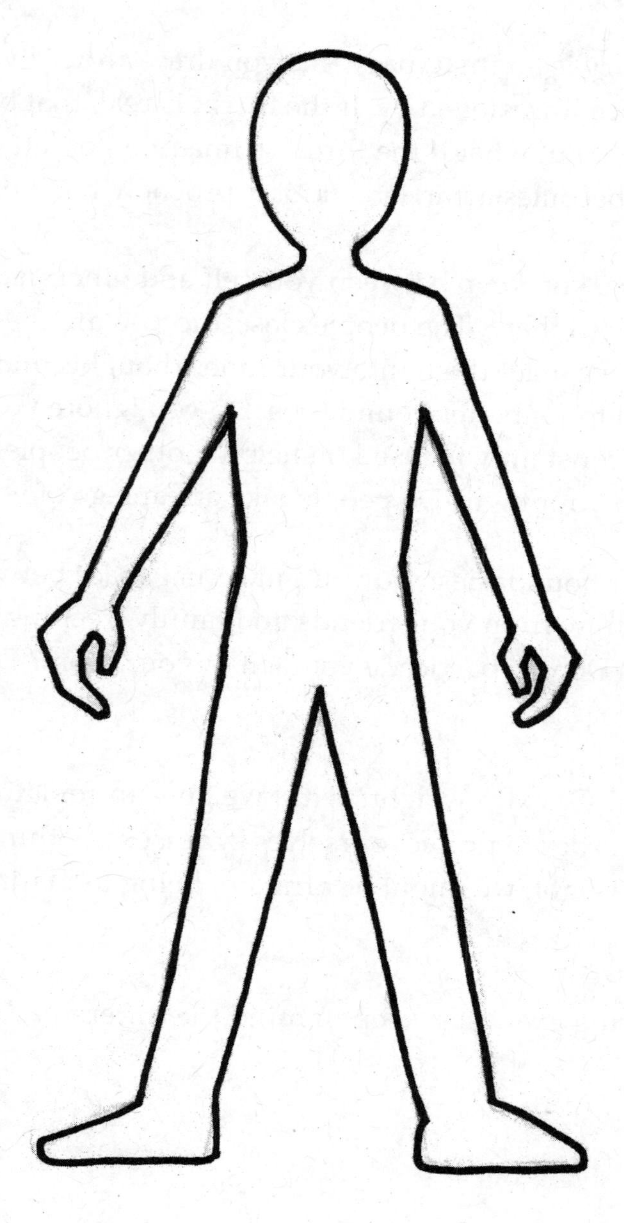

2. Using the space below, draw where you feel safest. Then, indicate where you feel safe having other people who are in your life. Who is in your inner circle? Who is in the next circle of your life? Which people do you keep in the outer circles of your life?

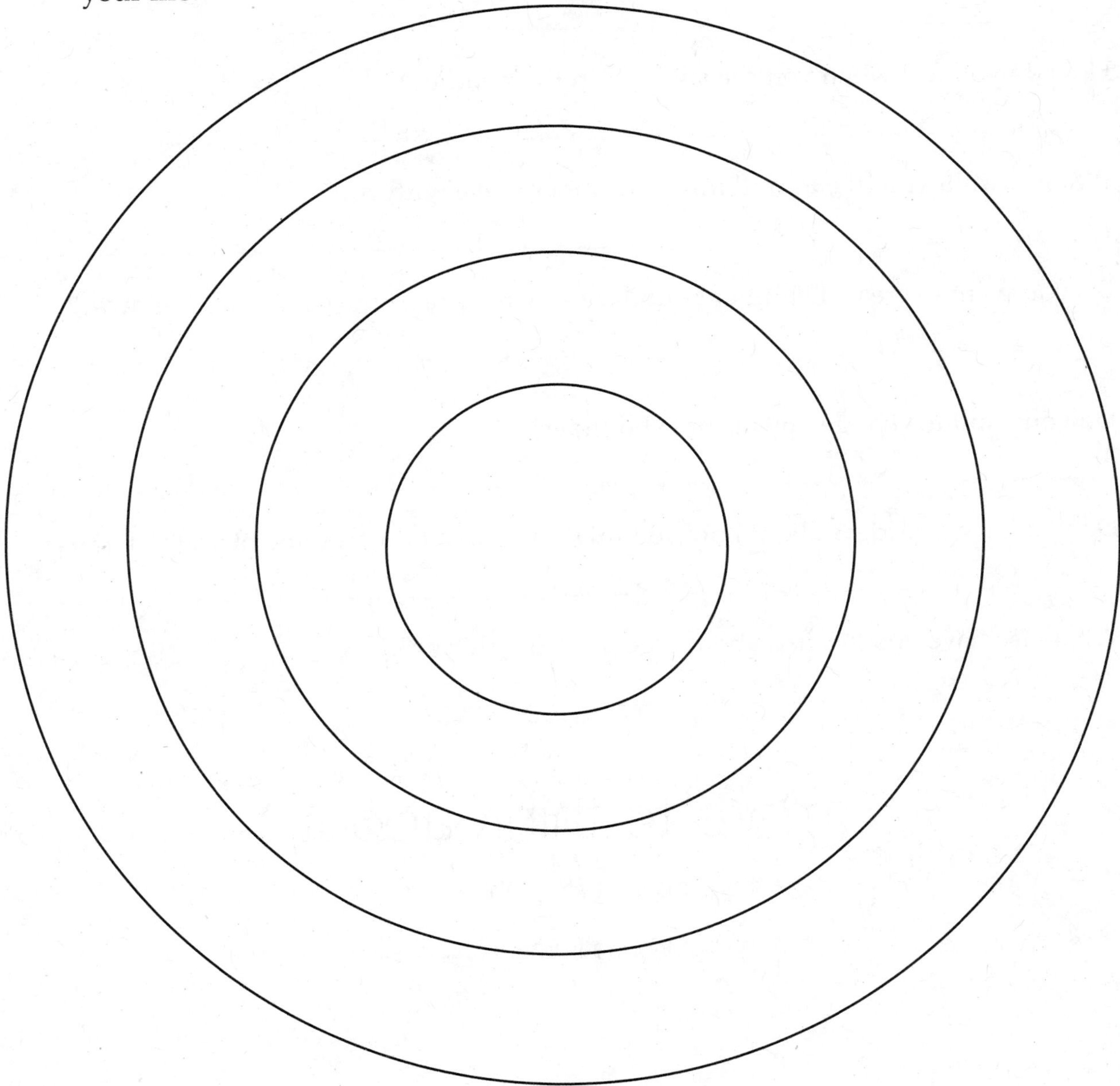

Indicate with colored arrows where you would *like* to move each of these people if you were feeling more comfortable with your own boundaries and safer in your body.

follow-up

Are you surprised by any of the boundaries you have drawn? ______________________

____

How do you feel when you see yourself in the middle? ______________________

____

Whom would you like to pull into your inner circle with you? ______________________

____

Do you want to create healthier boundaries by moving some people farther away?

____

Do you want to change any of these boundaries? ______________________

____

Do you have any ideas about how you might like to let down some of your barriers?

____

What else have you learned about yourself from this exercise? ______________________

____

more to think about

- What can you share with your parents from this exercise?
- What can you share with your friends from this exercise?

understanding your own fairy tale 5

focus

This exercise will help you understand your personal myths and how they relate to your life.

In many stories, children read about the prince who saves the helpless princess. This recurring theme has created generations of girls, and perhaps boys, who believe that we all need someone to rescue us. The theme of "happily ever after" is another fairy-tale idea that has influenced how we view our relationships and has made us wish for happy endings.

1. Write a fairy tale about your idealized life. Before you start, think about these questions:
    - What will your happy ending be?
    - Who is going to rescue you?
    - What will happen to cause a conflict in your life?
    - Who is your archenemy?
    - Who will magically be there to support you?
    - What do you need to survive the conflict?
    - What will happen to you after you have everything you want?

My Fairy Tale

Title ____________________

There once was a ____________________

who lived ____________________.

And she felt ____________________.

Sometimes she liked to ____________________.

Then ____________________.

And next she met ____________________.

Something terrible happened: ____________________.

And her archenemy ____________________.

Then an amazing magical thing occurred: ____________________.

And she was rescued by ____________________.

A secret was revealed: ____________________.

In the end, ____________________.

And *after* the "happily ever after": ____________________.

2. Think about the fairy tale that was your favorite when you were growing up.
   - What fairy tale was it? ____________________

     ____
   - What did you like about it? ____________________

     ____

     ____
   - How did that story help you create the fairy tale you just wrote? ____________________

     ____
   - What character do you most relate to in your fairy tale, and why? ____________________

     ____

     ____
   - What would be an alternative ending for your fairy tale? ____________________

     ____

     ____

follow-up

How do myths in our culture help us, and how do they hurt us? ______________________

____

____

What fairy-tale character do you most relate to? ______________________________

____

____

Why is it important to think about what follows the happily-ever-after ending of fairy tales?

____

____

____

How do you think these ideas apply to your eating disorder behavior? _____________

____

____

____

more to think about

- Can you write a new fairy tale that focuses on you as a different character?
- Who do you want to be?

family dinner table 6

focus

This exercise will show you how what happens during family meals can affect your eating disorder behaviors.

While the dinner table can be a warm and comfortable place where your family gathers and talks about their day, it can also be a place for a quick, and possibly stressful, meal. The dinner table offers a window into the dynamics in your family and how they affect you.

How your family deals with food is an important part of exploring eating disorder behaviors. One way to examine your family members' attitudes about food and eating is by drawing your family dinner table. This drawing can also help you look at issues between you and other members of your family.

what you'll need

Colored pencils or thin markers
Two large sheets of drawing paper

Draw a picture of your family at the dinner table. Take as much time as you need and include as much detail as possible about the table, the people, yourself, and the background.

When you have finished your drawing, answer the questions below. Keep in mind that there are many different ways to talk about your drawing, and there are no right or wrong answers.

Who is sitting at the table with you? ____________________

Where are you in relation to other family members? ____________________

What are the spaces like between family members? ____________________

Who is hidden by the table or chairs? ____________________

Is anyone missing from the table who should be there? ____________________

What are you doing? ____________________

What is everyone else doing? ____________________

Is there food on the table? ____________________

What are the family members eating? ____________________

Are you eating? ____________________

What do the colors suggest to you? ____________________

Which people are drawn in similar colors? ____________________

Which people are similar in size or shape? ____________________

Looking at this drawing, what are your feelings? ____________________

____

What would you change about this table? ____________________

____

follow-up

What do you think your observations about your family dinner table mean?

____

____

What do you think your drawing says about how you developed your eating disorder behaviors?

____

____

What would you like to change about the way you interact with your family?

____

____

more to think about

- Can you draw a picture of your family at the breakfast table? Is it different? How?
- Can you draw a picture of how you would like your family to be at the dinner table? How is it different?
- Can you share your drawing with someone in your family?
- Can you ask members of your family to draw their own pictures of the family dinner table?

7 healing overeating

focus

This exercise will help you understand compulsive overeating and find other behaviors you can substitute.

For many people, overeating is a comfort that helps them feel less anxious. Finding other ways to cope with anxious feelings is an important part of recovering from compulsive overeating.

The questions below explore what you might feel like if you stopped overeating. Answering them can help you understand why you overeat and how you can stop. It can also tell you what to do as an alternative, to prevent overeating in the future.

If I can't eat whatever I want whenever I want it, I will feel:

1. ______________________ 3. ______________________

2. ______________________ 4. ______________________

If I can't eat whatever I want whenever I want it, here's what I will probably do instead:

1. ______________________ 3. ______________________

2. ______________________ 4. ______________________

If I can't eat whatever I want whenever I want it, I will probably look:

1. ______________________ 3. ______________________

2. ______________________ 4. ______________________

If I can't eat whatever I want whenever I want it, I'll probably have to change:

1. ______________________ 3. ______________________

2. ______________________ 4. ______________________

If I can't eat whatever I want whenever I want it, these things will not change:

1. ____________________ 3. ____________________

2. ____________________ 4. ____________________

I wish I could eat whatever I want whenever I want it because:

1. ____________________ 3. ____________________

2. ____________________ 4. ____________________

If I can't eat whatever I want whenever I want it, I will miss:

1. ____________________ 3. ____________________

2. ____________________ 4. ____________________

follow-up

What seems to be the common theme among all your answers? ____________________

____

____

Do you see a pattern in your feelings about overeating? ____________________

____

____

more to think about

- How do you feel about depriving yourself of what you want?
- What do you think you can do to help you feel like you are giving yourself a gift instead of depriving yourself?

8 body image scale

focus

The Body Image Scale can help you understand how you are feeling at any given time about your body and about yourself.

Sometimes we blame the way our bodies look for how we feel about our lives. It is important to be aware of what we feel, not just what we look like. What we feel is not always connected to how we look.

The Body Image Scale is an important tool to determine what you are feeling and what you are at risk of doing to your body. If you score high on the Body Image Scale, congratulations! You are probably doing pretty well in your life and taking good care of yourself. If you score low on the Body Image Scale, you need to seek help because you may be in danger of harming yourself.

This scale can show you the progress you are making. Make a copy and keep it in your journal or hang it in your room or locker. Use it often to check where you are. If you are sinking low on the scale, ask yourself why and talk with someone.

Body Image Scale

Circle the number of the sentence that describes how you are feeling about yourself at this moment.

1. I have very extreme dislike for my body.
2. I have extreme dislike for my body.
3. I dislike my body.
4. I occasionally dislike my body.
5. I have average feelings about my body.
6. I am comfortable with my body sometimes.
7. I am usually comfortable with my body.
8. I am almost always comfortable with my body.
9. I like my physical appearance.
10. I am totally accepting of my body.

follow-up

Use the Body Image Scale only as a suggestion of how you feel about your body. It's a tool to help you become more self-aware, but it won't tell you how you are doing in your recovery from eating disorder behaviors.

When you are at different places on the Body Image Scale, try to identify what you feel about your life and your relationships—not about your body. You may notice that what you feel about your body changes depending on what's going on in your life. You'll learn to deal with your feelings rather than turning them into negative thoughts about your body.

more to think about

- How do you think your feelings about your body affect your eating disorder behaviors?
- When you are feeling better about your body, what is usually the reason? If your reason is related to your weight, think of five alternative reasons that have nothing to do with how much you weigh or what you look like.

if my body parts were colors 9

focus

This is an exercise to get you to think about your body. Sometimes art activities can give you a new way of looking at yourself.

Having an eating disorder can make you feel like you are living your life from the neck up. You may never want to be in your body at all. Yet your body can be a very colorful and amazing place to live. Can you look at your body as separate parts, each with a different color? Taking the time to focus thoughtfully on your body in this way will help increase your awareness of how you feel about it

Color this outline as if it were a picture of you. Use a different color for each body part. Then fill in the blanks on the following pages, indicating what color you chose for each body part and why. Think about what the colors mean to you.

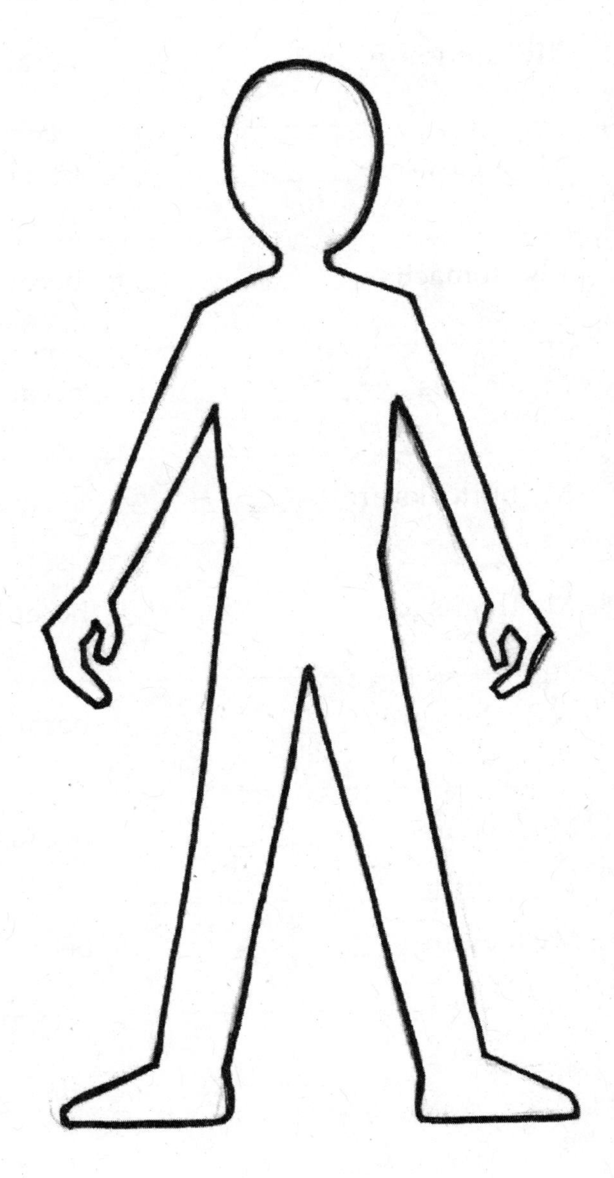

My face is ______________ because ______________________________
____.

My neck is ______________ because ______________________________
____.

My arms are______________ because ______________________________
____.

My hands are______________ because ______________________________
____.

My breasts are______________ because ______________________________
____.

My stomach is______________ because ______________________________
____.

My back is______________ because ______________________________
____.

My buttocks are______________ because ______________________________
____.

My thighs are______________ because ______________________________
____.

My calves are______________ because ______________________________
____.

My feet are______________ because ______________________________
____.

My toes are______________ because ______________________________
____.

follow-up

How do you feel about your body parts, now that they are colors? Go back and write a feeling next to each description.

more to think about

- Without focusing on your weight, what would it take to get your body parts to be the colors you'd like them to be?
- What attitudes would you have to change in order for it to happen?

10 kickback effect

focus

This exercise will teach you ways to change your eating patterns and make it easier for you to control your behaviors.

Most people can stick to a weight-loss plan or a diet for about three weeks. After the first three weeks of giving up unhealthy eating, most people experience what can be called the "kickback effect." They decide that their plan is no longer going to work; their willpower runs out, and they return to their previous eating habits. Dieting is a temporary solution to a long-term problem. To make changes that are permanent and healthy, you can't depend on willpower alone. You also have to understand your feelings, and this understanding can prevent the kickback effect.

Change works on the three-step rule:

- It takes three days for your body's cravings to end when you stop doing something addictive.
- It takes three weeks to start a new routine and determine if you like it.
- It takes three months to break a habit.

If you regularly eat processed sugars, simple carbohydrates, and junk foods, your body is used to the spike in your blood sugar level that takes place when you digest large amounts of sugar or simple carbohydrates. You actually crave sugar and the "high" it gives you; this craving is the number one symptom of an addiction.

It takes three days of no sugar and regular amounts of protein, which regulates your blood sugar, for your body to stop craving sugar highs. After three weeks, you can get used to a new food plan. By eating healthy amounts of food every few hours, you'll stabilize your blood sugar and protein levels, allowing your body to feel content. At the end of three months, healthy eating patterns will become a habit, and occasional treats of sweet desserts or snacks can be added into the food plan. Food will no longer be used as a way to deal with emotions.

Keeping the three-step rule in mind, answer the questions below:

What unhealthy eating behavior am I willing to give up for *three days?* ____________

How do I feel about giving that up for three days? ____________

What new routine will I commit to for *three weeks*, to see if I like it? ____________

How will that new routine affect my life, and how will I feel about that change? ____________

____

What habit do I hope to break over the next *three months*? ____________

How will I know I have broken that habit? ____________

follow-up

After three days, record what you are feeling and what changes you have made:

____

After three weeks, record what you are feeling and what changes you have made:

____

After three months, record what you are feeling and what changes you have made:

____

more to think about

- What will be different in your life?
- How will you feel different about yourself?
- Without your earlier habits to lean on, what feelings might come up in you?

11 perfectionism

focus

This exercise will help you be more reasonable in what you expect of yourself.

Perfection: Do you know anyone who is perfect? Is there anything in the world that is perfect? When you try to be perfect, you set up expectations that can never be reached, which leads you to a constant feeling of disappointment. Striving for a perfect weight, a perfect body, or a perfect anything will only lead to feeling bad about yourself. It can start a spiral into eating disorder behaviors.

In the space below, draw a perfect circle.

What do you notice about how hard it is to draw something perfectly? ____________

____

Even beautiful flowers are not perfectly shaped. In the space below, draw a flower, making sure that it is not perfect.

What do you like about the flower with all its imperfections? ____________________

____

follow-up

Twelve-step recovery programs use slogans that help addicts and alcoholics be realistic in their expectations and feel less anxious. These slogans can help you, too. Choose one or two from the examples below and write them down where you can see them every day. Repeat them to yourself whenever you find yourself thinking you need to be perfect.

- Easy does it.
- One day at a time.
- Keep it simple.
- First things first.

more to think about

- Think about your expectations for yourself. If you get a B instead of an A as a school grade, are you happy?
- What about your expectations for other people?

12 your food plan

focus

This exercise will help you make a plan for healthy eating. It will also help you see how your eating habits can affect you emotionally.

Sometimes we become so out of touch with what our bodies need that we don't even know when we are hungry or full. Eating too many or too few calories throws your body out of balance and can lead to emotional and physical illness. Letting go of unhealthy food patterns and adding healthy foods is important for eating disorder recovery and prevention. A nutritionist or registered dietitian can help you understand what a balanced meal plan is and how many calories you should be eating each day.

Your food intake affects how you feel emotionally. Make copies of this worksheet and record what you eat and how you feel every day for three weeks.

Date	What I ate	How I felt emotionally
Breakfast		
Lunch		
Snack		
Dinner		
Snack		

What do you notice about the connection between what you eat and your emotions?

____

____

With whom can you share this activity to see if you are on a healthy food plan?

____

____

follow-up

The third week of a new food plan is crucial, and you may feel like giving up. At the third week, ask yourself:

What should I change at this point? ______________________________

____

What should I give up because it isn't working? ______________________

____

Why do I feel these things are not working? _________________________

____

What should I keep that is working for me? _________________________

____

What can I do to make the things that are working for me continue in the next three months?

____

____

more to think about

In three months, look at this worksheet again and record your thoughts and feelings.

your family portrait 13

focus

This exercise will help you see that what happens between members of your family can affect your eating disorder behaviors.

Let's take a look at your current family structure. It is likely that stress generated within your family contributes to your eating disorder behaviors. If you can better identify what is happening, you will have a clearer language to communicate your feelings to your family. One way to do this is to draw a family portrait.

what you'll need

Colored pencils or thin markers
Two large sheets of drawing paper

Draw a picture that includes you and all the people in your immediate family. Show each person in your drawing doing something.

Answer the following questions about your family portrait:

Where are you in the family portrait? ___

Where are your family members in relation to you? ___

Who is grouped with whom? ___

Is there anyone who seems cut off or separated from everyone else? ___

Who has their eyes open? Closed? ___

Who has hands? Who has feet? ___

Does everyone have a mouth? Ears? ___

Is anyone blocked by an object? ___

Where are the kids in relation to the parents? ___

Where are the food-related objects: stove, table, food, and so on? ___

Where are they on the page in relation to you? To other family members? ___

Which people are drawn in the same colors? ___

What do you think the colors mean? ___

How are you different from everyone else? ___

Who is nearest you? Farthest from you? ___

Is everyone the same size? Who is largest? Smallest? ___

What interests you the most about your family portrait? ___

What would you like to change about your drawing? ___

What do you think the portrait says about your eating disorder behaviors? ___

___

___

follow-up

Looking at your drawing, what can you say about how your family interacts?

____

If you changed yourself, what would change in your family portrait?

____

more to think about

Here are some common interpretations that might interest you:

- Mouths can represent having a voice. Who has a voice in your family and who is not speaking?
- Ears can represent the ability to hear what is going on. Who is listening and who is not listening?
- Closed eyes can mean that someone is trying to ignore what is happening.
- Having no hands can mean a feeling of no control.
- Having no feet can mean feeling stuck, with no control over moving in one's life.

Can you think of other things in your drawing that might represent what is going on in your family?

14 abstract self-portrait

focus

This exercise will help you become more aware of your individuality and understand that who you are inside is the real you.

Every day, we are bombarded with television, radio, and magazine ads that focus on plastic surgery, dieting, clothes, and make-up. The media focus on appearance is so strong that many of us fall into the trap of identifying our outside appearances as the "real" us and forgetting who we really are on the inside.

So how do you focus more on who you are inside? How are you different from everyone else? How do you find the real you? One way is to remember that you are more than your appearance.

what you'll need

Colored pencils or thin markers
Two large sheets of drawing paper

Using only lines, shapes, and colors, draw an abstract portrait of yourself. Do not include your eyes, hair, legs, arms, or other parts of your body. Instead, your drawing should represent who you are on the inside—how you feel, what you think, what you are made up of—but not what you look like. Fill up the entire page.

On a second sheet of paper, draw another abstract self-portrait. This time, draw what you want to be like inside. Remember, this is not a drawing of your body or your face.

Then answer the following questions:

What do you like about your first drawing? ______________________________

____

What did you find hardest about drawing yourself abstractly? ______________

____

What colors did you use most often in your first drawing? ________________

____

What do you think those colors mean? ______________________________

____

How do you feel about your second drawing? __________________________

____

How do the shapes, lines, and colors differ in both drawings? Why are they different?

____

____

What would you have to change about yourself to get from the first drawing to the second?

____

____

What do you think these drawings have to do with your eating issues?

____

follow-up

If you drew an abstract self-portrait every day, what do you think you would see?

____

____

Whom can you share your drawings with? ______________________________

more to think about

- How does this drawing help you more clearly identify who you are as a person?
- If you were to draw another abstract self-portrait in a few hours, it would be different. What does that tell you about the nature of who you really are?

what I want to tell my parents (if only they would listen) 15

focus

This exercise can help you work toward an open and honest relationship with your parents. You'll learn to communicate your feelings and be more accepting of their feelings.

If you could tell your parents how you really felt, what would you say? You can use this exercise to express your feelings and share what you've written with your parents.

Using the letter on the following page, write to your mom, your dad, or both, telling them how you really feel. Find a time when your parent(s) can listen and talk without interruption, and read your letter out loud. Be willing to listen to feedback. If the feelings get too intense, take a break and come back later.

Dear ______________,

Sometimes I find it hard to tell you how I feel. I know you want to help me, and you may not be sure about how to do that. This letter can be our first step in understanding each other.

When I say something, can you please repeat it back to me so I know you got it? I will then tell you either, "Yes, you got it" or "No, that's not quite it," and repeat what I said until I've made myself clear. It will mean so much to me if I can tell that you are really listening, instead of rushing to give me advice.

Lately, I have been feeling ______________________________. When you ______________________________, it makes me feel ______________________________.
And I know that when I ______________________________, it makes you feel ______________________________. Some things I need you to know about what I am going through right now are ______________________________
____.
I really need some help with ______________________________________.
Some ways that you can help me are ______________________________
______________________________. Some things I think we need to change are ____.
If there are things you think need to change, I am open to listening.

I really need to know that you hear my feelings and I want to hear yours. I know that may be hard for both of us and I am committed to having an open and honest relationship. Can we do that together?

Thanks for listening.

Love,

____

follow-up

Talking to your parents can be hard and frustrating, both for you and for your parents. Having a format for expressing your feelings, like the letter you wrote above, sometimes makes it easier to say what you need to.

What was it like to write your letter? ______________________________

____

____

What was it like to talk to your parent about your letter? ______________

____

more to think about

- Who else do you need to write a letter to?
- Can you use this format to write a letter to someone else?

16 negative self-talk

focus

This exercise will help you turn negative thoughts into positive ones. When you learn how to do that, you will feel better about yourself.

We can't always be positive. Sometimes we say negative things about other people and the way they look; sometimes others say negative things about the way we look. These messages become part of our self-talk, or the words we use in our own minds when we talk to ourselves about the way we look.

Self-talk can be either positive or negative. "I look good today" is a positive message; "I look fat and ugly today" is a negative message. Self-talk can influence how our day is going, what our mood is, and even how we act toward other people.

Our feelings about our bodies can change drastically every second of the day. For example, imagine how you feel standing next to someone who is short and petite in comparison to you. Now picture yourself standing next to someone who is twice your size. Although your body size hasn't changed, chances are you have a totally different feeling about yourself. By changing our negative thoughts, we can change how we feel about our bodies.

1. Write any negative thoughts you have about any part of your body or your body as a whole.

___

___

2. Write any messages, good or bad, you have heard about your body. If possible, list the people you heard these messages from.

___

___

3. Write any messages you heard as a child about other people's bodies.

___

___

4. How did these messages make you feel about yourself?

___

___

5. For each negative thought you wrote in response to the first question, write one positive thought. Try to pick messages that you really believe are true. For example, "I hate my hair" could be "My hair has a nice natural wave."

___

___

follow-up

Are there people you would like to talk to about the messages you heard about your body? You may want to say something like:

> "I have been working hard on my self-esteem. I realize that some of the negative thoughts I have about my body come from my past. Will you talk about that with me?"

During and after the conversation, remember to maintain positive thoughts about your body.

more to think about

Positive self-talk is the beginning of a positive body image. Learning to see yourself realistically, and not how others see you, is an important part of learning to rid yourself of negative body thoughts and change the way you judge your body.

about food and weight loss 17

focus

This exercise will help you understand your ideas about food and weight loss, if compulsive overeating is a problem for you.

Answer each question as honestly as you can. You can complete the worksheet in one sitting or take your time and answer one question a day.

To me, food represents ______________________________.

All my life, I've used food as ______________________________.

What will help me lose weight is ______________________________.

Looking at my body makes me feel ______________________________.

I am angry at ______________________________.

The feelings I use food to bury are ______________________________.

Food helps me avoid ______________________________.

I love food because it ______________________________.

Sometimes I am afraid to eat because ______________________________.

Parts of my body that I love are ______________________________.

To lose weight, I am willing to sacrifice ______________________________.

Strengths that will help me lose weight are ______________________________.

What has helped me in the past is ______________________________.

follow-up

I realize now that food has been a way for me to ________________________________
____.

Being more aware of how I have used food to avoid my feelings has helped me because
____
____.

more to think about

- Draw what you think being healthy would feel like, not what it would look like.

relaxing your body 18

focus

In this exercise, you'll learn different ways to relax your body. Learning how to relax will help you when you feel stressed.

Can you tell when you are stressed? Do you know what your body feels like when it is tense? When it is relaxed? Studies have shown that we can actually decrease our blood pressure, slow down our pulses, and lower our heart rates by relaxing. Relaxation techniques can actually change what happens in our minds and bodies and ultimately, can even change what our bodies look like! Knowing how to control stress in our bodies helps us to be physically and emotionally healthier, and it can prevent us from using self-destructive eating and purging habits to deal with our uncomfortable feelings.

Practice these exercises once a day. You can record them on a tape player, have someone read them to you from this page, or read the worksheet carefully and practice what you remember.

Exercise One

1. Find a comfortable place to sit or lie down and focus all your attention on your body.
2. Slowly breathe in through your nose and out through your mouth, ten times.
3. Focus all your attention on your feet. Imagine the bottoms of your feet open like trap doors. Picture all the stress in your body flowing out from the bottoms of your feet and into the floor.
4. Imagine stress flowing out from the bottoms of your feet, into the floor, and down into the earth. The stress flows like water into the dirt, through the mud and rocks, and into the molten lava at the center of the earth, dissipating like steam into the Earth's core.
5. Focus on your calves, letting go of all stress.
6. Focus on your shins, relaxing, letting go of all tension, and feeling it drain out through your feet and into the floor.
7. Relax your knees and your thighs. Feel the muscles in the back of your thighs and the front of your thighs, the muscles that carry you around all day, as they relax. Feel the flow of relaxation all the way down to your feet.
8. Feel the base of your spine as it settles into the surface beneath you. As you are pulled down by gravity, feel how relaxing that is.

Exercise Two

1. Breathe into your belly, filling it with air. Relax it fully as you exhale.
2. Relax your lower back. Moving up your spine, relax the rest of your back.
3. Feel your shoulders relax. Feel them pull down toward the Earth. Let all the tension roll off them and flow into the ground.
4. Breathe in and exhale. Let all the tension from your shoulders and your back flow down into the Earth, letting it all go and feeling what it is like to relax.

5. Relax your arms—your upper arms, your biceps and triceps, your forearms; relax your hands and all your fingers. Feel the stress flow down your arms and hands, flowing out of your fingers and down into the ground.

6. Relax the back of your neck where it meets your spine. Relax your jaw. Relax your tongue. Take a deep breath, feeling all the tension flow out of your jaw muscles.

7. Relax your forehead. Feel the tension smooth out of your forehead. Let all the worry lines smooth out of your face, feeling the stress and tension leave your face and neck, flow down your shoulders, and over your arms, leaving your body and flowing down into the ground as you exhale.

Exercise Three

1. Take a deep breath. Exhale. Relax.

2. Take another deep breath. Let the feeling of relaxation smooth over your entire body, soothing your muscles, relaxing your joints.

3. Feel light and warmth soothe and cover your entire body and flow into the floor.

4. Breathe and relax; feel your body. Think of your sore, stuck places, and breathe warmth and light into those stuck places. Relax and let go.

5. Feel the tension drain through your body and into the floor.

6. Take a deep breath into your core. Relax and let go.

7. Fall into a relaxed state of consciousness; sleep if appropriate.

8. Come to, fully relaxed and aware and comforted in your body.

follow-up

What were some things you noticed that made you realize your body was tense?

____

____

Which relaxation exercise worked the best for you? Explain why.

____

____

What part of this exercise can you practice at home? At school?

____

____

Which parts can you teach your friends? Your siblings? Your parents?

____

____

How can relaxation help you with healthy eating?

____

____

more to think about

- You can relax your body throughout the day, as you need to.
- The signal to your body will be a deep breath in and out, letting go of all the stress of the day.
- How often can you commit to practicing these exercises each week?

affirmations 19

focus

This exercise will help you think more positively about yourself. Having a positive body image will make it less likely that you will turn to self-destructive eating disorder behaviors.

What happened to the little kid you used to be? You had total control over that person's body. You could run and jump and play with other kids, and your body did exactly what you told it to. When you wanted to run, it ran. If you wanted to rest, it stopped. With all the hormonal changes of adolescence, your body may seem to have a mind of its own. Sometimes it responds in ways you feel totally powerless over. You can feel great in your body one day and terrible the next; it is all part of growing up.

Feeling unhappy in your body can lead to negative thoughts that make you feel even worse about yourself. These thoughts can cause you to feel depressed, afraid, or exhausted, and they can lead to self-destructive behaviors. Repeated often enough, these thoughts become part of your consciousness. They replay in your mind even when you are not aware of them and affect your physical, emotional, and spiritual health.

1. Complete the following sentences with the first responses that come to your mind:

   The worst thing about my body is ________________________________.

   The best thing about my body is ________________________________.

   What I don't like about my body is ________________________________.

   What I appreciate about my body is ________________________________.

   My body is not cooperating, because it ________________________________.

   My body has always been ________________________________.

   What I have come to accept about my body is ________________________________.

   I feel the following about my body:

   My body is ________________________________.

   My body is ________________________________.

   My body is ________________________________.

   My body is ________________________________.

   My body is ________________________________.

   My body is ________________________________.

   My body is ________________________________.

   My body is ________________________________.

   My body is ________________________________.

   My body is ________________________________.

2. Positive affirmations are statements written in the present that can help you change your thoughts about yourself. If you said, "My body is fat and ugly," a positive affirmation to correct that message would be, "My body is beautiful and perfect." You may not believe an affirmation at first, but by repeating it and focusing on it, you can turn your negative thoughts into positive ones.

Looking at the comments you wrote about your body, notice how many negative messages are running through your mind. Go back and rewrite these messages, turning them into positive affirmations.

My body is ____________________.

My body is ____________________.

My body is ____________________.

My body is ____________________.

My body is ____________________.

My body is ____________________.

My body is ____________________.

My body is ____________________.

My body is ____________________.

My body is ____________________.

3. Writing affirmations and reading them is an important part of "rewiring" your mind to eliminate the negative messages you have been feeding yourself. Pick out one affirmation from the list above, and write it out ten times.

My body is ____________________.

My body is ____________________.

My body is ____________________.

My body is ____________________.

My body is ____________________.

My body is ____________________.

My body is ____________________.

My body is ____________________.

My body is ____________________.

My body is ____________________.

4. Post several affirmations—either your own or ones from the list below—where you will see them often: on your bathroom mirror, in your locker at school, over your desk. Let them sink in and begin to change the way you think about yourself. Remember, you don't have to believe them at first. Eventually your subconscious will teach itself to like you and be gentler with you!

AFFIRMATIONS

- ✔ I approve of my body exactly the way it is.
- ✔ I love my body and all its parts.
- ✔ My body is healthy and strong.
- ✔ I am loving and gentle with my body.
- ✔ I am grateful for my healthy and happy body.
- ✔ I am happy to be good to my body.
- ✔ My body is wonderful just the way it is.
- ✔ I love my figure and accept its changes.
- ✔ My body is beautiful in its uniqueness.
- ✔ I love the way my body works.
- ✔ I am happy with my looks.
- ✔ My body is perfect just the way it is.
- ✔ My body is the perfect container for me.
- ✔ My body is healthy and beautiful.

follow-up

Put your sheet of affirmations on the wall above your bed or in your bathroom so you can look at it every day. Each morning, choose an affirmation that works for you. Throughout the day, read it aloud, write it down, and say it to yourself.

more to think about

Look back at some of the negative messages you have been telling yourself. It's not likely you would ever say those things to your best friend or to your sister, so why would you say them to yourself? The next time you find yourself playing negative messages in your head, be as gentle and loving with yourself as you would be with your best friend.

I am ... 20

focus

This exercise will help you understand what is special and unique about you.

As teenagers, we often want to be just like everyone else. To become healthy adults, we must first look at how we are similar to, and different from, others. Then, we can begin to shape ourselves as individuals.

1. Fill in the blanks after the words, "I am...." It is important that you do it quickly and without a lot of thought so that your answers are spontaneous.

I am ______________________________

I am ______________________________

I am ______________________________

I am ______________________________

I am ______________________________

I am ______________________________

I am ______________________________

I am ______________________________

I am ______________________________

I am ______________________________

I am ______________________________

I am ______________________________

I am ______________________________

I am ______________________________

2. Read your answers aloud, as if you were reading a poem. Record or videotape yourself as you read. As you replay it, notice how it describes you as a unique person.

3. Notice which statements were negative messages and which ones were positive. Mark each negative message with a minus sign and each positive message with a plus sign.

4. For each statement, ask yourself:
   - Has someone else told me this message about myself? Who was it?
   - How have these messages affected my body image?

5. Look at the first five statements you wrote. If they are negative, can you change them?

6. Notice your last five statements. These are ones you may have had to really search for. Are they more real than the first five? Why?

7. Choose five positive messages and write them as affirmations. For example, if the statement is, "I am nice to my younger sisters," the affirmation might be, "I am a nurturing, caring person, and I am good with children."

   I am ______________________________

   I am ______________________________

   I am ______________________________

   I am ______________________________

   I am ______________________________

follow-up

Share your "poem" with a person you feel close to. Try this exercise again in several weeks or months and see how you have changed. It is amazing how we can grow in short periods of time!

more to think about

- As you grow stronger in your sense of self, your "I am" messages may grow more positive.
- Notice that the more positive and supportive your messages to yourself are, the more positive and supportive your messages to those around you become.
- We all need affirmation to grow, and we have to give it to ourselves first.

21 family patterns

focus

This exercise will help you look at how members of your family handle conflict and how family conflicts affect your eating behavior.

Think back to the worksheet 6, "Family Dinner Table", earlier in this book. All families have their own ways of relating to each other. The way your family handles conflict can also affect you, and you may react to conflict with self-destructive eating patterns.

The questions below will help you see how your family may have affected your eating patterns.

What are some of your dysfunctional eating patterns? ______________________

____

What would happen to the rest of your family if your eating behavior became more stable?

____

____

What emotions are most commonly expressed in your family? How are they expressed?

____

____

How do you resolve conflict in your family? ______________________

____

How would you describe the energy in your house at mealtime? ______________

____

When you are in a conflict with a family member, how does that affect your eating patterns?

____

____

When there is conflict in the family, how does that affect the family's eating pattern?

____

When you are upset or angry, how do you express yourself?

____

follow-up

Look at the answers you gave above. What patterns do you notice at home?

____

Are there ways your family deals with conflict that make it hard for you to have a healthy emotional balance? ____

____

How can you handle conflict without turning to dysfunctional eating patterns?

____

____

more to think about

- Can you share any or all of your answers with your family?
- If you do share and there is conflict as a result, how will you handle it?

22 pop star

focus

This exercise will help you realize that you are an individual and do not have to conform to society's idea of the ideal body.

Several years ago, magazines portrayed women in popular situation comedies as having tiny, extremely underweight bodies, with large and seemingly overdeveloped heads precariously balanced on their frames. These women were nicknamed "lollipops." We know now that being so underweight is not only unattractive, it is a warning sign that a young woman is in serious physical danger. But women are still in competition to maintain the "ideal" body, whether it is the lollipop body or the curvier body of some of today's pop stars. Our media continues to foster the idea that happiness depends on having the body they deem ideal.

Think about the stars in music, the models in magazines, and the actresses in movies and television. In the space on the left, draw the body that you think is the ideal portrayed in the media. On the right, draw what you think your body looks like.

How is your body different from the cultural ideal of today? ______________________

____

How is your body the same as or close to the cultural ideal of today? ______________

____

What do you do to try to force your body to be like the ideal of today? ___________

____

How does that hurt you physically, emotionally, and spiritually? _________________

____

What might be unattractive about the cultural ideal of today? What don't you like about it?

____

____

List ten things you like about your body. Don't think too hard; just write!

1. ______________________ 6. ______________________

2. ______________________ 7. ______________________

3. ______________________ 8. ______________________

4. ______________________ 9. ______________________

5. ______________________ 10. ______________________

follow-up

What problems do you think pop stars idealized by the media might have?

____

____

What do pop stars have to do to stay popular?

____

____

____

more to think about

- How is your life easier than the life of a TV sitcom character?

23 be a tree

focus

This exercise will help you understand that people are unique and do not have to compete.

No two trees in the forest look alike. If we expect that they will all be different and don't see one as better than another, why do we compare our bodies to someone else's?

Find a comfortable place to sit or lie down. Read this exercise and practice as you read it. Then try it with your eyes closed.

> Be a tree.
>
> Feel your roots.
>
> Spread your branches.
>
> Feel the wind in your branches.
>
> Know that you are grounded in the earth and nothing can tip you over.
>
> You can sway with the storms and grow toward the sun.
>
> You have an endless supply of energy coming up from the ground. Whenever you need it, you can send your roots down and feel that energy coming up into your trunk and spreading out into your branches and leaves.
>
> When the world feels tough, let your branches absorb the light from the sun. Know that you can be a tree among trees.
>
> Appreciate for a moment that no two trees are alike. Every tree in the forest is different, and yet without every tree, there would be no forest.
>
> Do trees compete to look the same?

follow-up

How does competing to look like everyone else work for you? ______________________

____

How does competing to look like everyone else work against you? __________________

____

Who told you that you had to look like everyone else? ____________________________

____

How would it feel to look like you do and know that that was good enough? ________

____

more to think about

- Practice being a tree whenever you feel competitive around your friends or in school. Spread your branches and be you. Remember, no two trees are alike.

24 "I'm not good enough" thoughts and how to stop them

focus

This exercise will help you cope when you start to have negative thoughts about yourself.

Do you ever have "I'm not good enough" thoughts? You may have those thoughts when you feel lonely or when you compare yourself to others. You may have them when you feel like your body should look different than it does.

If your "I'm not good enough" thoughts had a face, what would it look like? Draw the face below.

If it had a voice, what would that voice sound like? ____________________

____

Does it speak about your body? If so, what does it say? ____________________

____

What would you like to say back to the "I'm not good enough" voice? ____________

____

What is it like inside your head when that voice is ruling your day? Draw what it feels like, using lines, shapes, and colors.

Draw what it would feel like inside your head if that voice were quiet.

Imagine you could tell that voice to stop talking. Would you yell, "STOP"? Would you shout? Describe how you would tell the voice to stop. ____________________

____

What can you picture in your mind to help you stop your "I'm not good enough" thoughts? It might be a stop sign or a soundproof wall or a police officer blowing a whistle. Draw that picture below.

follow-up

Your "I'm not good enough" thoughts can lead to self-destructive behaviors, like bingeing, purging, or restricting food. Learning to recognize these thoughts is an important step in gaining a sense of control over your patterns of self-destruction. When you have an "I'm not good enough" thought, you can do the following:

- Recognize it.
- Tell it to stop.
- Picture something that will stop it.
- Write or draw about it.
- Talk about it.

more to think about

These steps will help you to get past your old behavior and move on to using new, healthy coping skills. You can take control of your recovery and move into the life you want to live!

whose body is this? 25
part I: I am unique

focus

This exercise will help you accept the type of body you have and recognize your similarities to family members who came before you.

No two bodies in this world have the same shape. Even identical twins have slight differences between them. Our unique shapes—the gentle slope of our shoulders, the broad, strong expanse of our hips, the roundness of our bellies—are all a result of the families we come from.

The cultural ideals in our society determine what we hold to be attractive. If you are growing up at a time when being tall and thin is the ideal, and your ancestors were short and stocky, you may feel uncomfortable with the short, stocky body you inherited. Looking at the models in magazines, you may feel hopelessly out of fashion. Realizing that no amount of dieting, plastic surgery, or magical thinking can change your heritage, can you love and accept yourself exactly as you are? Whether your relationship with your mother and other female relatives has been smooth or problematic, can you acknowledge the strength of the women in your family who came before you? Can you feel the connection your body gives you to them?

In this visualization exercise, you will get in touch with all of your female ancestors. Let yourself experience the feeling of connection you have to all the women before you!

1. Close your eyes and take several deep breaths into the center of your body. Relax into your chair, grounding your feet on the floor and letting gravity pull you into the Earth.
2. Imagine yourself in a safe and relaxing place in nature. There is beauty and tranquility all around you, as far as your inner eye can see.
3. Now imagine that your mother stands behind you, supporting you, holding you up. You lean on her slightly.
4. Behind her stands her mother. You both lean back on her, and she supports you both gently. You relax. Breathe.

5. Imagine the three of you relaxing against your great-grandmother, as she stands behind you. You are all in a line, one behind the other.
6. Now imagine the four of you relaxing against your great-great-grandmother standing behind you.
7. Slowly picture all the women in your ancestral line standing behind each other, all holding you up. Visualize these women, reaching back in time to the first woman you can imagine.
8. See these women as strong, capable, beautiful, and unique. Feel what that feels like. Breathe.
9. Open your eyes. Write down any thoughts or feelings you may have in your journal or the Notes pages at the end of this workbook.

Think about the countries your ancestors came from. Then focus on your body and its separate parts. Part by part, identify whom you most closely resemble in your family. For example write, "My legs are most like my mother's. She came from Poland."

My hair is most like my ______________________'s. She came from ______________________.

My face is most like my ______________________'s. She came from ______________________.

My eyes are most like my ______________________'s. She came from ______________________.

My mouth is most like my ______________________'s. She came from ______________________.

My shoulders are most like my ______________________'s. She came from ______________________.

My arms are most like my ______________________'s. She came from ______________________.

My breasts are most like my ______________________'s. She came from ______________________.

My belly is most like my ______________________'s. She came from ______________________.

My hips are most like my ______________________'s. She came from ______________________.

My legs are most like my ______________________'s. She came from ______________________.

My ankles are most like my ______________________'s. She came from ______________________.

My feet are most like my ______________________'s. She came from ______________________.

I am also like my female ancestors in these other ways:

____

____

____

____

follow-up

Were you able to see all the women in your ancestral line? ____________

How did it feel to lean against them as they supported you? ____________

Can you draw a picture of what this visualization was like for you?

more to think about

After you complete these exercises, say the following affirmations aloud:

- I am powerless to change some things about my body.
- I appreciate the parts of me that resemble my ancestors and make me unique.
- I honor my relatives, living and dead.
- The way I look is special and connects me to the women in my family lineage.

Add further affirmations if you can. Remember, affirmations are positive and in the present. For example, "I am beautiful like my Aunt Jeanne" or "I love my Native American heritage."

whose body is this? 26
part II: interview

focus

This exercise will help you see how your family history has influenced your eating behavior and body type.

In Worksheet 25, we began to explore the connection between heritage and body make-up. How our bodies look is not only a result of how we eat and exercise, but also a result of what we inherit. To continue, you'll interview female family members to learn about their body images.

You can use the introduction below to explain to your relatives that you are learning about women in your family and their body images. If you prefer, you can introduce the interview in your own words. Bring a notebook; you may also want to record the interviews on audiotape or have someone videotape them.

Body Image Interview

Thank you so much for taking the time to let me interview you. I am interested in hearing about the women in our family and how they have felt about their bodies. I realize you may not know much about our family several generations back, and that's okay; please just answer my questions the best you can. If you have any pictures of you now or when you were younger that you could share with me, I can make copies and return the originals. When I've finished collecting information, I'll share what I've learned with you.

1. How do you feel about your body today?
2. How did you feel about it when you were my age?
3. Where were you born? In what year?
4. What was it like growing up as a girl where you lived?
5. What was the ideal body when you were a teenager?

6. How closely did you feel you fit that ideal?
7. Did you feel pretty when you were a teenager?
8. Did you feel like you fit in?
9. How did your mother feel about her body when you were growing up? How did you know?
10. What do you think the ideal body was when she was a teenager? Was she like that or unlike that?
11. Where did your mother grow up?
12. Where did your grandmother grow up?
13. What was the ideal body when she was growing up? Was she like that or unlike that?
14. Who do you think you most resemble, and why?
15. Who do you think I most resemble, and why?

follow-up

Write up the interviews and put them into a binder, with pictures or drawings of all of your female relatives. Share these stories with your relatives. Someday, you may even have your own daughter to share them with!

more to think about

- Adapt this interview form and use it to learn about your friends, your teachers, and other people you know. You can interview the men in your family as well to learn about their body images.
- Ask all of your friends to answer some of these questions and bring the forms home to their own relatives. Meet to discuss the results.

whose body is this? part III: family tree 27

focus

This exercise will help you recognize your connection to your family and realize that eating disorder behaviors are often rooted in family history.

Each of us has an effect on our appearance, but we have also inherited a set of unchangeable factors from our parents and their parents before them. These factors influence what we look like. By looking at your family tree, you can begin to understand the impact of those who came before you.

Before you can create a family tree, you'll need to gather information by talking with relatives, both men and women, about their recollections of your family. Start by asking your parent, grandparent, aunt, or uncle to sit down with you and make a list of as many relatives as they can think of. Put lists together for both sides of your family.

You can use the questions below as a guide and also ask for other information you are interested in knowing about your family and its history.

- How old are these relatives or how old were they when they died?
- What did they die of?
- What country were they born in, and what country are they in now?
- Did anyone in our family have anorexia or bulimia? Was anyone obese?

Here are some additional questions you may be curious about:

- Who were the athletes in the family? What sports did they play?
- Who played an instrument?
- Were there any artists in our family? Doctors? Farmers?
- Did anyone serve in the military? Where and when?
- Are there any feuds between family members?

- Were there any divorces? Stepfamilies?
- Are there any stories in our family of quirky or interesting relatives?

Think of other questions you may be curious about. Remember to be patient and give people time to think and go back into their memories. Finally, ask for family pictures that you can copy and return.

When you have compiled as much information as possible, you are ready to begin creating your family tree.

what you'll need

Colored pencils or thin markers
#2 pencils with erasers
A large sheet of oak tag
A glue stick
A photo of yourself
Photos of relatives
Small stickers

1. Draw a tree with the base of the trunk at the bottom of the paper. Add branches stretching up to the top and corners of the page.
2. Find a baby picture of yourself, or draw one based on your parent's recollections, and glue it on the trunk of the tree.
3. Fill in the names of your parents above you on the trunk, just where the branches begin. Include their names and current ages. Add pictures of them if you have them.
4. On a branch to the left above your parents, add your mother's parents' names with their ages or the ages that they were when they died. If they have passed away, indicate that with a thin root to the ground or up to a cloud in the sky

above your tree. Include anything you have that reminds you of them: pictures, flags of their country of origin, medals, and so on.

5. On a branch to the right of your parents, repeat step 4 for your father's parents.
6. If you have brothers or sisters, write in their names and ages to the left and right of your picture. Include pictures.
7. If you have nieces or nephews, include them below their parents. Write their ages as well.
8. Beneath your grandparents on both sides, include any children they had and their ages. These people are your aunts and uncles, your parents' brothers and sisters.
9. Beneath or next to your aunts and uncles, include the names and ages of your cousins.
10. Now continue up the tree and out, adding your great-grandparents on both sides with whatever information you have about them.
11. Expand with any great-aunts, great-uncles, and second cousins.
12. If you have further information, continue up and out, adding great-great-grandparents and more.

    Note: If there have been divorces and remarriages in your family, show couples who are together now. Connect children to their biological parents with a green line and to their stepparents with a blue line. Possibly confusing, but it is common!

Now that you have compiled an actual picture version of your family tree, you are ready to look at eating disorder patterns. Place a sticker next to the name of any relative who has had an eating disorder issue, including anorexia, bulimia, or obesity.

Using colored pencils or markers, color your family tree. Hang it up on a wall or mount it on a wooden board or foam core.

follow-up

How did it feel to interview your relatives for your family tree? ______

______

What were some things you noticed about your family when you began compiling notes from your interview? ______

______

What did you learn about your similarities to many of your family members? Your differences? ______

______

How many people in your family tree did you discover had eating disorder issues?

______

______

Do you think that your family's history is unique or that most families have similar issues in their background? ______

______

Are there any family members or situations that you feel embarrassed about? ______

______

Which part of your family tree do you feel particularly connected to? Are they relatives who are alive today, or are they ancestors? ______

______

more to think about

Invite your relatives to a Family Tree party to share the family tree you have created. Take pictures of them as they enjoy it, and send copies to family members who can't be there.

from mother to daughter 28

focus

This exercise will help you communicate with your mother and become aware of ways that you are alike.

In every generation, there is a body shape considered to be ideal. Some years, it is fashionable to be thin; some years, it's the style to have curves. And in every generation, many are not going to fit the standard of perfection. A mother who has a problem with her own body image is more likely to have a daughter with eating disorder behaviors. And that mother's problem may have come from her mother.

Ask your mother the following questions:

1. If you had to describe how you feel about your body in a few words, what would you say?

   ____

2. What do you want to pass on to me about how I should feel about my body?

   ____

3. What issues about your own body do you need to work on?

   ____

4. What did your mother value about women's bodies?

   ____

5. How did your mother feel about dieting?

   ____

6. What messages did your mother pass down to you about women's bodies?

   ____

Now, imagine your mother looking at herself in a mirror. What is she saying?

____

____

What is her body language saying? ______________________________

____

follow-up

How do you think the answers your mother has given affect you? __________

____

What messages have you learned from your mother about how to feel about your body?

____

____

____

more to think about

- Can you share what you learned in this worksheet with your mother?
- If you have a daughter someday, what would you like her to know about your feelings about your body and about how she should feel about her own body?

frustration scale 29

focus

This exercise will help you cope with frustration and stress. You can use the techniques you'll learn to avoid eating disorder behaviors.

Tension is the building up of energy that leads to stress. Stress is the uncomfortable feeling we have when things feel out of our control. When we feel powerless to change the things that create our stress, frustration results. Sometimes we deal with frustration by relying on temporary, and often unhealthy, coping mechanisms.

Using the Frustration Scale, you can learn to delay acting out with self-destructive behaviors and to use positive coping skills instead. When you notice signs of tension or stress, use this scale to determine your frustration level. At certain points on the scale, you'll find suggestions for positive coping skills and, at the end, an explanation of how to use those skills. With practice, you will automatically know what to do when you recognize where you are on this scale!

Frustration Scale

Circle the number that corresponds to how you are feeling at the moment.

1. **Calm**
   Your body is relaxed; your breathing is slow.

2. **Slightly tense, but feeling good**
   Your body is slightly tense and your breathing a little more rapid than usual, but you basically feel relaxed and happy.

3. **Somewhat tenser, but in a good way**
   Your breath is slightly rapid, and your muscles are tense.

4. **Tense and feeling some stress**
   You may be tapping your finger or shaking your foot.
   ✔ Find a stress reducer.

5. **Somewhat stressed**
   Your shoulders, stomach, or lower back may feel tight.
   ✔ Find a stress reducer.

6. **Really stressed and getting frustrated**
   You are thinking more unhealthy thoughts and feeling more uncomfortable in your body.
   ✔ Take a time-out.

7. **Feeling pretty frustrated**
   Everything is bothering you. Your body is feeling tight and uncomfortable. You may feel pain and find it hard to relax or slow down your breathing.
   ✔ Take a time-out.

8. **Growing more frustrated**
   Your body is very uncomfortable. You may feel tension in your chest and find it hard to catch your breath, or your breathing may be rapid. You may be clenching your fists or your jaw. You may have a headache or backache. Your shoulders may be hunched or sore.
   ✔ Talk with someone.

9. **Really stressed**
   You are fighting with everyone around you. You feel like—or may even be—throwing things or punching walls. You want to do something self-destructive. You might feel like yelling or blowing up.
   ✔ Use your tools.

10. **Stressed to the max**
    Your frustration has affected your health, and you have gotten sick or acted out. You are feeling over the edge and may feel shame or remorse for some self-destructive act.
    ✔ Use your tools.

Positive Coping Skills

Positive coping skills are behaviors that can help you deal with uncomfortable feelings in a healthy way.

Find a Stress Reducer

To reduce stress, try meditating or doing a visualization. Work on a journal entry, draw a picture, or call a friend. You can also use positive affirmations.

Take a Time-Out

Time-outs are important stress reducers for everyone. They are a good way for you to relax for a few moments and reduce your own frustration.

Outside is a good place to take time-outs, if possible. Give yourself a limit—two minutes? Five? Ten? Sit and do nothing but focus on your breath, the sky, or a tree for a specified period of time. When your time-out is over, reevaluate where you are on the Frustration Scale.

Talk with Someone

If you are at a crucial point, find someone to talk with. Are your parents around? Can you tell someone how you are feeling? Pick up the phone and call a friend. Call your therapist. If you can't find someone to talk with right away, open your journal and write down how you feel. Write a letter or an e-mail to someone, even someone imaginary, like your future self. Telling someone how you are feeling will help you reduce your stress; then go back and see where you are on the scale.

Use Your Tools

At the end of this workbook, you will find additional tools you can use to keep yourself from acting out self-destructively.

follow-up

After you have practiced using positive coping skills, reevaluate where you are on the Frustration Scale. How has your frustration level improved? ______________________

____

When you are more frustrated, are you also more likely to use eating disorder behaviors? ____

____

Where on the Frustration Scale are you when you start thinking about acting out your eating disorder behaviors: 5, 6, 7? What can you do to decrease your frustration when it approaches that level? ____

____

Can you spot different levels of frustration in the people around you? What are your family members like at a 6 or 7? Do they ever get to 8, 9, or 10? Can you talk with them about how that makes you feel? _______________________________________

____

more to think about

Share this scale with your family so that they know the language you are using when you talk about the Frustration Scale. Let them know that when you get to a 6 or 7, it is time for you to take a time-out.

what makes life worth living? 30

focus

This exercise will help you think about the positive aspects of being a woman.

You cannot be creative and self-destructive at the same time. Creating something new shows your intention to move forward and expresses your need to grow. Creativity and self-destruction are two opposing forces, which is why art is so healing.

what you'll need

A large, sturdy piece of paper or cardboard
(or a piece of wood is okay if it is sanded and smooth)
A glue stick or white glue
Scissors
Magazines, photos, and other print materials
Natural materials like shells, leaves, flowers, twigs, sand, and so on
Fabric scraps, buttons, beads, and so on
Shellac

Make a collage that shows what makes you feel alive. Include images, words, and materials that represent what gives you hope and makes life worth living.

Glue what you have chosen onto your paper, filling the entire surface, even overlapping some materials. When the collage is entirely dry, spread a thin layer of shellac or white glue over the surface of the collage images. White glue, if thin enough, will dry clear and create a hard and clear surface for your collage that will protect the art and keep the edges from curling up. Display your collage where you will see it every day.

follow-up

Is there a central theme that seems to appear in your collage, showing what makes life worth living for you? ___

Did anything that appears self-destructive find its way into your collage? ___

___

How can you change it? ___

___

How did you feel while you were making your collage? ___

___

Did you lose track of time or forget about your problems for a short time? ___

___

With whom can you share your collage? ___

more to think about

- Remember, you cannot be creative and self-destructive at the same time.
- When you feel like doing something harmful to yourself, like bingeing or purging, do something creative. Make a collage!

vision box 31

focus

This exercise will give you more practice in expressing yourself creatively. It will help you think about the type of person you would like to be and the type of world you would like to live in.

Long ago, people thought the world was flat, and they were afraid they would fall off if they went too close to its edge. They could not imagine Earth as we know it. Today we see the world quite differently, and we are all influenced by our worldviews. We create our environment and our reality by believing in the vision we hold to be true.

What vision do you hold to be true about your world? Do you believe it is a gentle, nurturing place that cares for you and that you can count on? Do you believe that you are alone and on your own? How do you see the world around you? And do you believe you can change it?

what you'll need

A sturdy box like a shoebox, of any size
A glue stick or white glue
Scissors
Magazines, photos, and other print materials
Natural materials like shells, leaves, flowers, twigs, sand, and so on
Fabric scraps, buttons, beads, and so on
Shellac

Create a collage that shows your vision of the world. Use the inside of the box to show your ideal self and the outside to show your ideal world. You can make your box as realistic or as whimsical as you like.

Here are some questions for you to think about in creating your vision box:

- What is your vision of an ideal world?
- What is important to you for your personal future?

- Focusing on the type of person you want to be rather than on your appearance, how do you see yourself in the future?

follow-up

What did it feel like to create your vision box? ______________________

____

What do you notice about your vision box as a whole?______________________

____

How is the inside different from the outside? ______________________

____

What are three things you notice about the inside? ______________________

____

What are three things you notice about the outside? ______________________

____

When you look at your vision box, what do you feel? ______________________

____

more to think about

- What do you need to change in your life right now to create the ideal world on the outside of your box?
- How much of what is in your ideal world is within your control?
- How much of your ideal self is already part of you? What do you need to do to appreciate that?
- With whom can you share your box?
- What do you want to say about your vision?

make a mask 32

focus

This exercise will make you more aware of your true self. It will help you understand whether you show your true self to the world or hide behind a mask.

We all wear masks. We put on a face for the outside world, depending on where we are and whom we are with. Sometimes we wear the mask of a grownup or the mask of a student or the mask of a child. We may wear so many masks that it becomes hard to remember who we really are! Only by discovering the masks that you wear can you begin to take them off. Who is your true self? Sometimes there are layers of masks, and it takes time to dig down to the true you.

Sometimes it's good to put on a mask and have a dialogue with yourself. When we truly look at all our different "faces," we can begin to understand what parts of us are real and what parts of us are only a defense against letting people get to know us. In this exercise, you will make masks that show your true self and the self you hide behind.

what you'll need

Cardboard, at least 8" x 11"
Popsicle stick or tongue depressor
A glue stick or white glue
Scissors or a craft knife
Thin markers
Decorative materials

1. Cut the cardboard into the shape of a face. Glue the stick to the bottom of the shape, or pierce the cardboard and insert the stick into the mask. Using scissors or a knife, make holes in the cardboard for eyes and mouth. If you prefer, you can draw the features.

2. Your creation should represent one of the masks you present to the world. Glue on any decorative materials that help portray this self.

3. Repeat the last activity, but this time, make a mask of your true self. Who have you been hiding? Can you show her in a mask?

4. Now put the first mask up to your face and look in a mirror, as you think about the answers to these questions:

   - What do you see?
   - If that mask were to say something, what would it be?
   - If that mask had a name, what would it be?
   - How has that mask helped you to protect yourself up until now?
   - How is the second mask different from the first?

follow-up

If the person each mask represents were to talk with you, what would she say? Talk with the mask on, and then take it off and talk back to her. Write down your conversation.

more to think about

- How can you use this worksheet to remind you that you don't always need to wear a mask?
- Notice when you are wearing your first mask out in the world. What can you do to make the situation safe enough for you to take the mask off?

focus

This exercise will help you become more aware of your feelings and how they affect you. Being aware of your feelings can help you avoid self-destructive eating behaviors.

We can react to our feelings in many different ways. We may communicate them appropriately, responding directly to others or to ourselves through creative expression. But when our feelings are too overwhelming, painful, or anxiety provoking, we may react by:

- Burying our feelings
- Focusing excessively on our bodies–counting calories, having negative body image thoughts, or having "fat" thoughts, and so on—to distract ourselves
- Acting out with self-destructive behaviors, such as purging

Being able to identify your feelings and recognize your way of reacting toward them is important in working toward a balanced and focused life. Many different emotions fall into the categories of mad, sad, glad, or afraid. Sarcasm, jealousy, and irritability are all "mad" emotions. "Sad" emotions include loneliness, grief, and regret, while contentment, peace, and cheerfulness are in the "glad" category. "Afraid" feelings include anxiety, nervousness, or panic. We all experience so many different emotions that sometimes it's hard to recognize what we are feeling!

Write down as many "mad" feelings as you can think of: ____________________

____

Write down as many "sad" feelings as you can think of: ____________________

____

Write down as many "glad" feelings as you can think of: ____________________

____

Write down as many "afraid" feelings as you can think of: ____________________

____

Having an idea of how you feel in any given moment is important to avoid acting out your feelings or burying them. Being aware of your emotions can help you express them in healthy ways. Take a moment to listen to your inner emotional state. How are you feeling right at this moment? Check all that apply:

❑ Afraid
❑ Aggressive
❑ Amazed
❑ Ambitious
❑ Angry
❑ Annoyed
❑ Anxious
❑ Apologetic
❑ Aroused
❑ Arrogant
❑ Ashamed
❑ Aware
❑ Bold
❑ Bored
❑ Brash
❑ Cautious
❑ Cheerful
❑ Confident
❑ Confused
❑ Content
❑ Curious
❑ Depressed
❑ Determined
❑ Disappointed
❑ Ecstatic
❑ Enlightened
❑ Enraged
❑ Envious
❑ Exasperated
❑ Excited
❑ Focused
❑ Frustrated
❑ Glad
❑ Grateful
❑ Grieving
❑ Guilty
❑ Happy
❑ Hopeful
❑ Hurt
❑ Incredulous
❑ Indifferent
❑ Innocent
❑ Intuitive
❑ Irritable
❑ Jealous
❑ Joyful
❑ Lonely
❑ Loving
❑ Mad
❑ Meditative
❑ Mischievous
❑ Moody
❑ Nervous
❑ Obsessive
❑ Obstinate
❑ Panicked
❑ Peaceful
❑ Perplexed
❑ Prayerful
❑ Regretful
❑ Relieved
❑ Sad
❑ Sarcastic
❑ Shocked
❑ Shy
❑ Smug
❑ Stoic
❑ Stubborn
❑ Surprised
❑ Sympathetic
❑ Thoughtful
❑ Thrilled
❑ Uncomfortable
❑ Withdrawn

follow-up

Each day, using the list above, choose five emotions you have felt. Write down those feelings in your journal or the Notes section at the end of this workbook. When you have an intense feeling, try to use the list to start a dialogue with the person your feelings are directed toward. Notice how that helps you avoid self-destructive behaviors. Write down any progress you think you have made by choosing to identify, feel, and express your feelings instead of burying them, avoiding them, or acting them out.

more to think about

- Checking your feelings regularly will help make you more aware of when you are most likely to turn to dysfunctional eating behaviors to avoid your emotions.

34 body image poetry

focus

This exercise will help you think about the positive aspects of being a woman.

In her poem *Phenomenal Woman*, Maya Angelou wrote about uniqueness of women and the beauty of their bodies. The poem opens with these lines:

Pretty women wonder where my secret lies.

I'm not cute or built to suit a fashion model's size....

Throughout the poem, Angelou refers to different qualities of women: the "span of my hips," "the joy in my feet," "the sun of my smile," "the need for my care." Her message is that women—women of all sizes and shapes—are phenomenal. Think about the words Maya Angelou has written. You many want to read the entire poem.

How does her message make you feel about being a girl? A woman? ______________

____

How does this message relate to your body image? To your self-esteem? ___________

____

In your journal or on the Notes pages at the end of this book, write a poem that shares your personal message about self-acceptance.

follow-up

Look for more poems that speak about women and body image. You can visit your library, find poems online, go to poetry readings, or browse in local bookstores. Find poets whose work you like, and read—get inspired!

more to think about

- Start a collection of poems that have an important message for you. They may be poems you've written or poems by others.
- Share your collection with someone close to you.

35 taking a time-out

focus

This exercise will help you build your self-control. When you are in control of yourself, you are less likely to turn to eating disorder behaviors.

Have you ever been so frustrated that you felt like you were going to explode? When we don't let ourselves take the time we need to regroup, our feelings can escalate and become overwhelming. At times, they may be too difficult to handle.

When you were a small child, your parents may have put you in time-out when you misbehaved. Time-out was a good way for you to relax for a few moments and reduce your own frustration. Now that you're older, time-out can still help when you reach the point where you don't know how to cope with your feelings. Time-out can give you the moments you need to experience your feelings, without worrying about how they affect others. Instead of burying your feelings or acting them out by reaching for eating disorder behaviors, you can give them a chance to pass.

Time-outs are an important way to reduce your stress, and they can be an alternative to overeating, undereating, or purging. If you practice this technique before you really need it, it will be easier to use when you do.

1. Remove yourself from a frustrating situation. Sit and do nothing but focus on your breath for a specified period of time. Try ten minutes at first. If you can't do ten minutes, try five. After your time is up, go back to the situation and see if your frustration level has decreased.
2. Writing during a time-out can help you get control of your feelings. While you are in time-out, write down everything you are feeling and thinking during that time. Try to write down everything you can, without worrying that someone else will read it or talk to you about it. Keep this thought in mind as you write: you can throw it all away when you are done.

Wait until twenty-four hours have passed before reading what you have written. Waiting may help you gain insight into your emotions and your urge to act out. And if at any time you want to throw out what you wrote, do it!

follow-up

Describe how you feel when you need a time-out. ______________________________

____

Are there situations when it may be difficult for you to take a time-out? __________

____

How can you make time-outs easier and more natural for you when you are upset?

____

____

more to think about

- How can you tell the people you are with that you need a time-out?

36 recognizing what you need

focus

This exercise will help you identify what you need. It will show you the connection between denying yourself food and denying yourself other things you need.

Is it hard for you to ask for what you need because you are afraid you won't get it? It may feel so much easier just to say, "I don't need anything!" But that can translate into a downward spiral affecting all your relationships. "I don't need anything" turns into "I don't need anything from you." Even your body gets involved in proving that you don't need anything from anyone, sending the message, "I don't even need food!"

Yet we all need food. And we all need other people. What else are you trying to prove that you don't need? It's likely that you do have needs that you have been afraid to tell others about. People can't read your mind. It's okay to tell them what you need. There's no guarantee that they will give it to you, but if you don't tell them, they don't even have a chance to meet your needs.

What are you trying to deprive yourself of? First, identify what you are denying:

1. I deny that I need ______________________________
2. I deny that I need ______________________________
3. I deny that I need ______________________________
4. I deny that I need ______________________________
5. I deny that I need ______________________________
6. I deny that I need ______________________________
7. I deny that I need ______________________________
8. I deny that I need ______________________________
9. I deny that I need ______________________________
10. I deny that I need ______________________________

Now name ten needs. They can be physical, emotional, or spiritual.

1. I need ______________________________
2. I need ______________________________
3. I need ______________________________
4. I need ______________________________
5. I need ______________________________
6. I need ______________________________
7. I need ______________________________
8. I need ______________________________
9. I need ______________________________
10. I need ______________________________

follow-up

Every day this week in your journal or in the Notes section at the end of this workbook, write down one thing that you need and one person who you think could help you meet that need. Each day, decide if you will ask that person to help or if you will try to meet the need yourself.

more to think about

- Do you normally focus on other people's needs?
- What is it like to think about your needs?
- Do you usually consider yourself weak if you ask for what you need?
- What might it feel like to be strong and still need things and people?

37 draw a bridge

focus

This exercise will help you move toward positive ways to cope. It will give you a healthy vision of your recovery.

Getting from one place to another is simple if we are talking about crossing a quiet neighborhood street. If we are talking about getting from dysfunctional eating patterns to healthy, balanced body image thoughts, getting from one place to another is much more complicated.

what you'll need

Colored pencils or thin markers
A large sheet of drawing paper

Draw a bridge from one side of the paper to the other. Add as many people or details as you like.

- Imagine that the left side of the bridge is your past, and draw where you are now.
- Imagine that the right side of the bridge is your future, and draw where you want to be.
- Underneath your bridge, draw what you are afraid of or what you are trying to conquer.
- Above your bridge, draw your image of the support and help you get from people in your life.

When you have finished your drawing, answer the questions that follow.

1. Describe what you see on the left side of your bridge. ____________________

   ____

2. Describe what you see on the right side of your bridge. ____________________

   ____

3. What is underneath your bridge? ____________________________________

   ____

4. What is above your bridge? ____

   ____

5. Is there anyone or anything on the bridge? ____________________________

   ____

6. If you could put yourself on the bridge, how far across would you be? ________

   ____

7. How does this drawing apply to your eating disorder behaviors? ____________

   ____

follow-up

In a few weeks, look at your bridge again. Where would you be on it now?

____

____

In a month or two, draw another bridge. What is on either side? What is above and below? Where are you?

____

____

____

more to think about

- Share the insights you gained with friends and family members. Then ask them to draw their own bridges and share their insights with you.

your emotional toolbox

At this point, you have many tools to keep you from relying on your past eating disorder behaviors. Instead of acting out self-destructively, you can pick a positive coping skill to help you to deal with uncomfortable feelings. This section reviews these tools in detail. On the next page, you'll find a handy list you can post to remind you of all the healthier solutions available to you.

Keep a Journal

A journal can be a safe place to write your thoughts and feelings. Sitting in a comfortable place, write down everything you are feeling. Begin with any emotions you notice and move on to any physical sensations you are aware of. Describe your surroundings in detail and move on to describing the relationships in your life.

Draw Your Feelings

Think about how you are feeling at the moment. If you were made up of lines, shapes, and colors, what would they be? Are you feeling soft and pastel? Are you more earth-colored right now? Do you take up the whole page or are you crouched in a corner? Your edges may be sharp and spiky or fuzzy, with smeared edges that you've rubbed with a tissue or cotton ball. Draw your feelings at this moment, feeling yourself relax as you express the moment on paper.

Create a Collage

You'll need a glue stick or white glue, scissors, and a large piece of construction paper, cardboard, or smooth wood. Using old magazines, find pictures and words to describe how you feel at that moment or how you would like to feel. Cut out the pictures and words or tear them, leaving the edges fuzzy. Glue the images onto your surface in a way that reflects your feelings. Fill the entire surface, even overlapping some images. When your collage is dry, paint a thin layer of white glue (or shellac) across the surface. If thin enough, the glue will dry clear and create a hard surface that will protect your collage and keep the edges from curling. On the back of your collage or in your journal, write about what you have done.

Use Relaxed Breathing

Slowly breathing in through your nose and out through your mouth, take five deep breaths. As you inhale, concentrate on filling your belly with air like a balloon. Then exhale, deflating the balloon, letting all the air out of your body. As you inhale, imagine breathing in peace and tranquility; as you exhale, imagine breathing out stress, tension, and anxiety.

Use Guided Imagery

Find a comfortable place to sit or lie down, and focus all your attention on your body. Slowly breathe in through your nose and out through your mouth, ten times. Focus all your attention on your feet. Imagine the bottoms of your feet open like trap doors. Picture all the stress in your body flowing out from the bottoms of your feet, into the floor, and down into the earth. The stress flows like water into the dirt, through the mud and rocks, and into the molten lava at the center of the earth, dissipating like steam into the Earth's core. Focus on your calves, letting go of all stress. Focus on your shins, relaxing, letting go of all tension, and feeling it drain out through your feet and into the floor. Relax your knees and your thighs. Feel the muscles in the back of your thighs and the front of your thighs, the muscles that carry you around all day, as they relax. Feel the flow of relaxation all the way down to your feet. Feel the base of your spine as it settles into the surface beneath you. As you are pulled down by gravity, feel how relaxing that is.

Talk with Someone

Can you tell someone how you are feeling? Talk to your parents or pick up the phone and call a friend. Call your therapist. Call a hotline. There are many hotlines that can help you in the middle of the night if you are awake and need to talk with someone. You can find their phone numbers in your phone directory or by calling information.

Write

Write a letter or an e-mail to a person you trust with your thoughts or with whom you'd like to share your feelings. Even if you never send it, tell that person what you are feeling and describe your life at this moment. You can also write to a person you make up, like an imaginary guide. What will you say about what you are going through? What questions will you ask? Imagine you get a response to your letter. What does it say? Or imagine you are your future self. Write a letter telling that future self how you are feeling. Ask your self where she is now and how she is doing. Can she give you any advice about getting through this time in your life? Can she reassure you that you will get through this time?

Take a Time-Out

Outside is a good place to take time-outs, if possible. Can you sit and do nothing but focus on your breath or the sky for a specified period of time? Try ten minutes at first. If you can't do ten minutes, try five. At the end of your time-out, see if your frustration level has decreased. Make sure you tell the people you are with that you are taking a time-out and will be back at the end of your specified time.

Use Positive Affirmations

Remember, positive affirmations are always in the present, not the future: "I am better," not "I will be better." You can use an affirmation like a key to turn off negative thoughts that are getting you down, but you don't actually have to believe it at the moment. What positive affirmation can you use right now? Can you tell yourself that you are okay right at this moment? Can you tell yourself, "I love and accept myself exactly as I am"? Repeat one positive affirmation twenty times and see how you feel.

YOUR EMOTIONAL TOOLBOX

Pick a tool that you think will work, and if it doesn't work, try another. Something in this toolbox will certainly work for you; it's just a matter of finding the right one for the situation you're in!

- ✔ Keep a journal.
- ✔ Draw your feelings.
- ✔ Create a collage.
- ✔ Use relaxed breathing.
- ✔ Use guided imagery.
- ✔ Talk with someone.
- ✔ Write.
- ✔ Take a time-out.
- ✔ Use positive affirmations.

NOTES

NOTES

NOTES

NOTES

NOTES

NOTES

NOTES

NOTES

Tammy Nelson, MS, has worked as a psychotherapist for over fifteen years. She is executive director and co-founder of the Center for Healing and Recovery in Norwalk, CT, and co-director and co-founder of the Ridgefield Center for Families & Children in Ridgefield, CT. Nelson is a licensed professional counselor, a registered art therapist, a licensed alcohol and drug counselor, and a certified Imago Relationships therapist. She resides in the New York City area, where she works in her private practice treating anorexia, bulimia, and other eating disorders using group and expressive therapy.

more instant help books

BEYOND THE BLUES

A Workbook to Help Teens Overcome Depression

US $14.95 / ISBN: 978-1572246119

COPING WITH CLIQUES

A Workbook to Help Girls Deal with Gossip, Put-Downs, Bullying & other Mean Behavior

US $14.95 / ISBN: 978-1572246133

STOPPING THE PAIN

A Workbook for Teens Who Cut & Self-Injure

US $14.95 / ISBN: 978-1572246027

THE ANXIETY WORKBOOK FOR TEENS

Activities to Help You Deal with Anxiety & Worry

US $14.95 / ISBN: 978-1572246034

THE DIVORCE WORKBOOK FOR TEENS

Activities to Help You Move Beyond the Breakup

US $14.95 / ISBN: 978-1572245990

available from

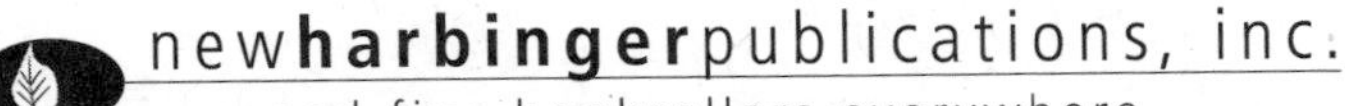

and fine booksellers everywhere

To order, call toll free **1-800-748-6273** or visit our online bookstore at **www.newharbinger.com**

(VISA, MC, AMEX / prices subject to change without notice)